Collins

First
Atlas
Learn with maps

Contents

The Contents page helps you to find the pages for different maps.

Finding school

This is Portmoak Primary School in Kinnesswood.

Portmoak Primary School
Kinnesswood
Kinross
KY13 9HT
Scotland
United Kingdom

Kinnesswood is in the British Isles.

British Isles

This book is an atlas.
An atlas has maps of our country
and the world.
They show where places are.
You can find out about the world.

British Isles: A view from space

This is a view of the
British Isles from space.

British Isles: Land, seas and islands

This is a map of the British Isles.
It shows land and water.
It shows islands.
It names some seas and
some islands.

Shetland Islands

N
W   E
S

Key

Land

Water

Orkney Islands

Outer Hebrides

Atlantic Ocean

North Sea

Isle of Man

Irish Sea

Anglesey

Ireland

Great Britain

Isle of Wight

British Isles: Some rivers and mountains

There are rivers in the British Isles.
There are hills and mountains.
The map shows and names some
of them.

N
W E
S

Key
River
Mountain

Atlantic
Ocean

North
Sea

North West
Highlands

Grampian
Mountains

River Tay

Lake
District

Pennines

Mourne
Mountains

Irish Sea

River
Shannon

Cambrian
Mountains

River
Trent

Macgillycuddy's
Reeks

River
Severn

River
Thames

British Isles: The two countries

The British Isles are made up
of the countries of the United
Kingdom and Ireland.
Each country has a capital city.
Each country has a flag.

Key

● Capital city

Dublin ○

Ireland

United

Kingdom

London ○

flag of the
United Kingdom

flag of Ireland

United Kingdom: Countries

There are four countries
in the United Kingdom.

Key

Countries

Scotland

Northern
Ireland

England

Wales

United Kingdom: Some cities

There are cities in the United Kingdom.
Cities are places where many, many
people live and work.
The map shows some cities.
It names them.

Key

Countries

City

Aberdeen

Scotland

Edinburgh

Glasgow

Northern
Ireland

Belfast

Newcastle
upon Tyne

Leeds

Manchester

Liverpool

Sheffield

Nottingham

Birmingham

Norwich

Wales

England

Cardiff

London

Bristol

Southampton

Europe: Some rivers and mountains

This is a map of Europe.
The British Isles is in Europe.
Europe is a continent.
There are rivers in the continent
of Europe.
There are hills and mountains.
The map shows and names some
of them.

Scandinavia
Mountain

North
Sea

British
Isles

Atlantic
Ocean

River
Rhine

River
Danube

The Alps

Pyrenees

N

W — E

S

Mediterranean

Africa

Key

~ River

Mountain

Asia

Ural
Mountains

*River
Volga*

Carpathian
Mountains

Caucasus

Black Sea

Caspian Sea

Asia

Sea

Europe: Countries and cities

There are countries and cities in the continent
of Europe.
Some countries are named.
Some cities are shown and named.

Norway

Oslo

North
Sea

Ireland   United
Dublin   Kingdom

Denmark

Copenhagen

Atlantic
Ocean

London   Netherlands   Berlin

Belgium   Germany

Paris   River   Pragu
Danube   Cze

France   Vier

Aust

Key

Countries

Capital city

River

Mountain

Portugal

Lisbon   Madrid

Spain

Zagr

Croa

Italy

Rome

Mediterranean

Africa

weden

Finland

Helsinki
ckholm
Tallinn
Estonia

Riga • Latvia

Lithuania
Vilnius

Minsk
Belarus

arsaw

oland

p.

ovakia

Budapest
ngary

Romania

Belgrade

Serbia

Bulgaria

Sofia

ana

lbania

Greece

Athens

Russia

Moscow

River
Volga

Kiev

Ukraine

Moldova

Chisinau

Bucharest

Black Sea

Caspian Sea

Asia

e a

Earth: Viewed from space

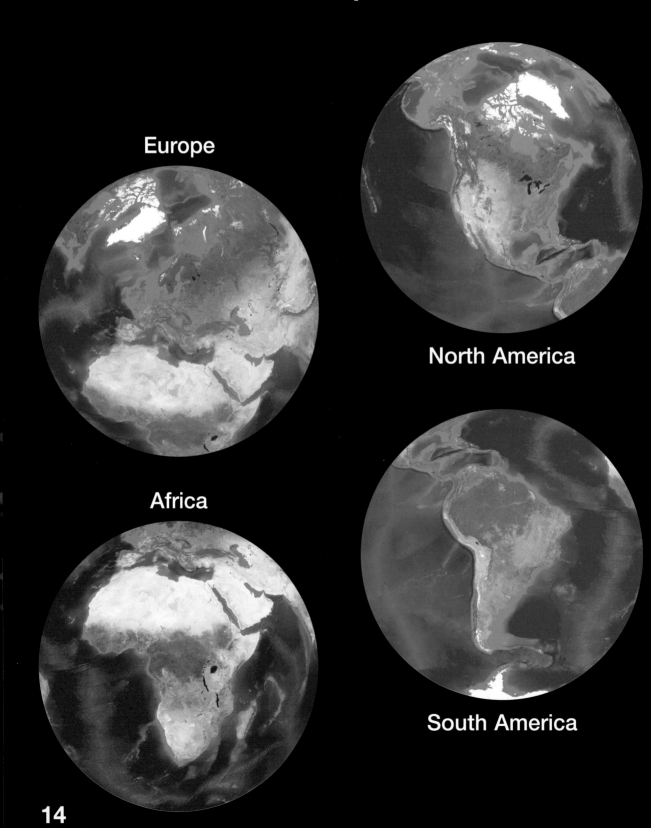

Europe

North America

Africa

South America

These views of the Earth from space
show each of the continents.
One view shows the Arctic Ocean.
Find the continent of Europe.
Each continent is an enormous
area of land.

Asia

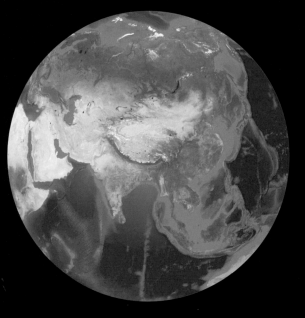

Oceania

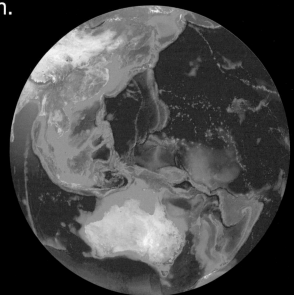

Antarctica

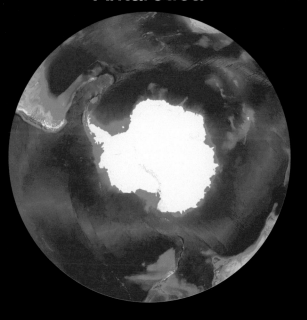

Arctic Ocean

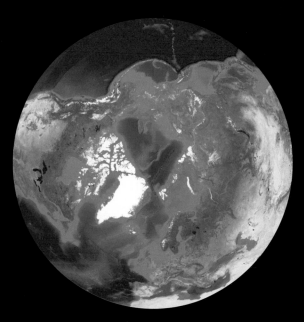

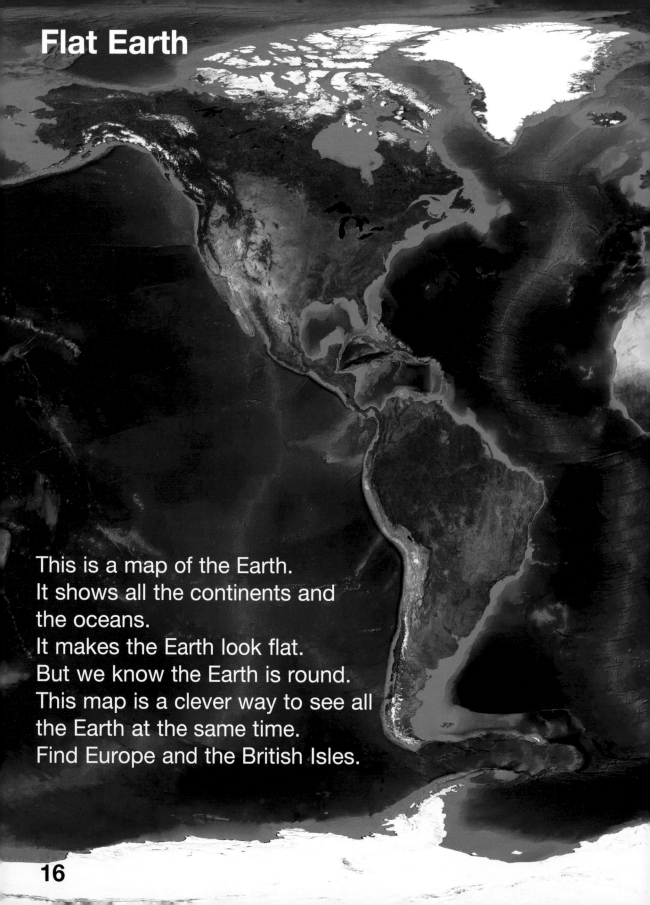

Flat Earth

This is a map of the Earth.
It shows all the continents and
the oceans.
It makes the Earth look flat.
But we know the Earth is round.
This map is a clever way to see all
the Earth at the same time.
Find Europe and the British Isles.

Use the other maps in the atlas to find out the names
of the other continents and of the oceans.

Asia: Countries and cities

Europe

Moscow

Russia

Africa

Ankara
Turkey

Caspian Sea

Astana
Kazakhstan

Ulan Bator
Mongolia

Iraq
Baghdad

Turkmenistan
Tehran   Ashgabat

Huang He

Beijin

Saudi
Arabia
Riyadh

Iran

Afghanistan
Kabul

Islamabad
Pakistan

China

Chan
Jiar

San'a
Yemen   Oman

Muscat

New Delhi
River
Ganges

Bangladesh
Dhaka

Myanmar

Hano

India

Nay Pyi Taw

Vietn

Thailand

Bangkok

N

W   E

S

Sri
Lanka

Ma

Key

Countries

Capital city

River

Mountain

Indian
Ocean

Kuala
Lumpur

18

Jakarta

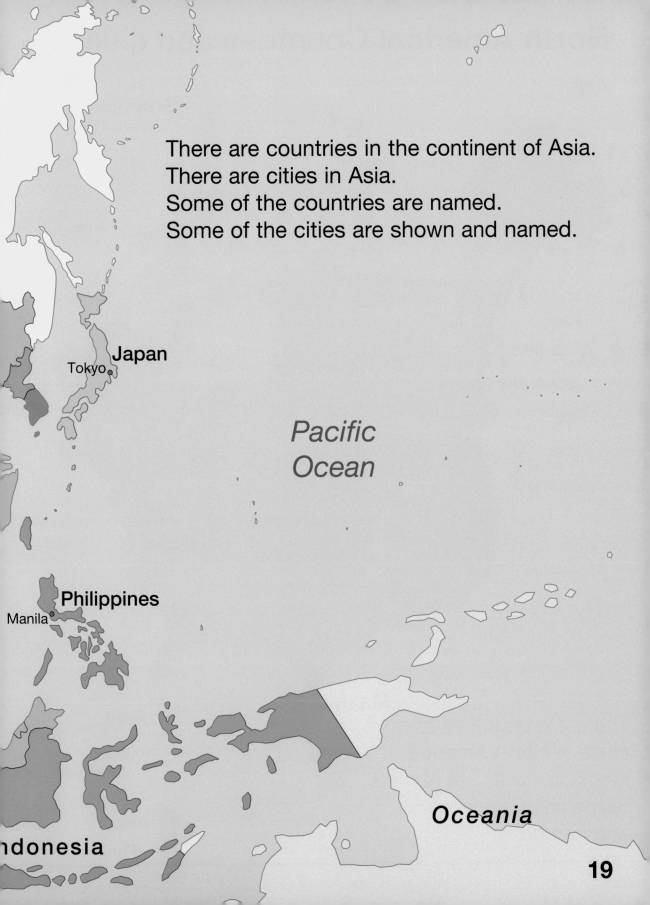

There are countries in the continent of Asia.
There are cities in Asia.
Some of the countries are named.
Some of the cities are shown and named.

Japan

Tokyo

*Pacific
Ocean*

Philippines

Manila

Oceania

Indonesia

19

North America: Countries and cities

Asia

Arctic Ocean

Greenland

USA

Nuuk

N
W   S

Key

Countries

• Capital city

• City

~ River

△ Mountain

Canada

Vancouver

Ottawa

San Francisco

Chicago

New York

Washington

Atlanti Ocean

Pacific Ocean

Las Vegas

United States of America

Los Angeles

River Mississippi

Mexico

Miami

Havana **Cuba**

Kingston

There are countries and cities in North America. Most countries are named. Some cities are shown and named.

Mexico City

Jamaica

Guatemala

Guatemala City

Nicaragua

Managua

Panama

San José
Costa Rica

Panama City

Sout Ameri

South America: Countries and cities

North America

Atlantic Ocean

Pacific Ocean

Caracas

Venezuela

Georgetown

Paramaribo

Guyana

French Guiana

Bogotá

Suriname

Colombia

Quito

Ecuador

River Amazon

Manaus

Peru

Brazil

Lima

La Paz

Brasília

Bolivia

Sucre

Paraguay

Rio de Janeiro

Asunción

São Paulo

Chile

Uruguay

Santiago

Buenos Aires

Montevideo

Argentina

Key

- Countries
- Capital city
- City
- River
- Mountain

There are countries and cities in South America. All countries are named. Some cities are shown and named.

Africa: Countries and cities

Europe

Asia

Key

Countries

Capital city

River

Mountain

Rabat
Algiers
Tripoli

Morocco

Algeria

Libya

Cairo

Egypt

River Nile

Mauritania

Nouakchott

Mali

Niger

Khartoum

Chad

Sudan

Eritrea

Asmara

Senegal

Dakar Bamako

Niamey

Ndjamena

Guinea

Conakry

Nigeria

Abuja

**Central
African
Republic**

**South
Sudan**

Juba

Addis Ababa

Ethiopia

Somalia

Mogadishu

Ghana

Accra

Cameroon

Bangui

Yaoundé

Libreville

Congo

Kampala

Uganda

Kenya

Nairobi

*Atlantic
Ocean*

Gabon

Brazzaville

**Democratic
Republic of
the Congo**

Kinshasa

Dodoma

*Indian
Ocean*

Tanzania

Luanda

Angola

Zambia

Lusaka

Mozambique

Harare

Antananarivo

N

W E

S

Namibia

Windhoek

Zimbabwe

Botswana

Gaborone

Madagascar

Pretoria

Maputo

There are many countries
in the continent of Africa.
Many countries are named.
Some cities are named.

**South
Africa**

Cape Town

Oceania: Countries and cities

There are countries in the continent of Oceania.
Many countries are islands.
Some countries are named.
Some cities are named.

Pacific Ocean

Asia

Papua New Guinea
Port Moresby

Yaren
Nauru

Bairiki
Kiribati

Solomon Islands
Honiara

Darwin

Vanuatu
Port Vila

Fiji
Suva

Australia

River Darling

Brisbane

Perth

Adelaide
Canberra
Sydney

River Murray

Melbourne

Hobart

Auckland

Wellington

New Zealand

Key

Countries

• Capital city

• City

〜 River

⌃ Mountain

Southern Ocean

23

Antarctica

This is the continent of Antarctica.
It is at the south of the Earth.
It is covered in ice.
There are no countries and no
cities in Antarctica.

Southern Ocean

Antarctic Circle

Weddell Sea

Antarctic Peninsula

Ronne Ice Shelf

Transantarctic Mountains

Antarctica

▶ South Pole

Amery Ice Shelf

Ross Ice Shelf

Ross Sea

Southern Ocean

Antarctic Circle

Key

☐	Ice shelf
☐	Ice on land
☐	Ice in sea
☐	Drifting ice

The Arctic Ocean

This is the Arctic Ocean.
It is at the north of the Earth.
Most of the Arctic Ocean is
covered in ice all year.
It is one of the oceans of the Earth.

Bering
Sea

Key

Ice on land

Ice in sea

Drifting ice

Arctic Circle

**North
America**

Arctic
Ocean

▶
North Pole

Asia

Baffin
Bay

Barents
Sea

Greenland

Arctic Circle

Iceland

Atlantic
Ocean

Europe

World: Continents and oceans

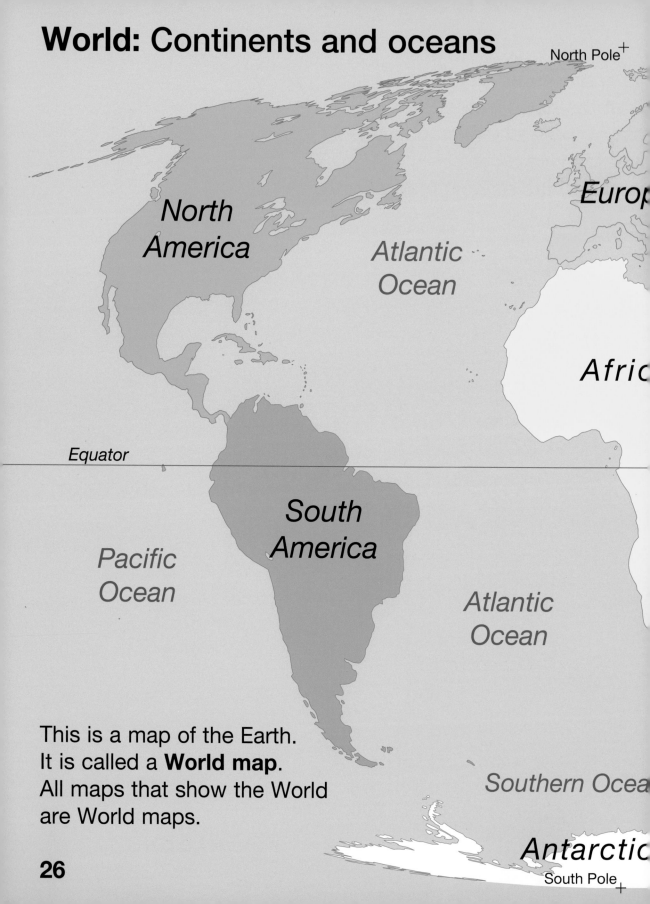

North Pole +

North America

Europ

Atlantic Ocean

Afric

Equator

South America

Pacific Ocean

Atlantic Ocean

This is a map of the Earth.
It is called a **World map.**
All maps that show the World
are World maps.

Southern Ocea

Antarctic

South Pole +

26

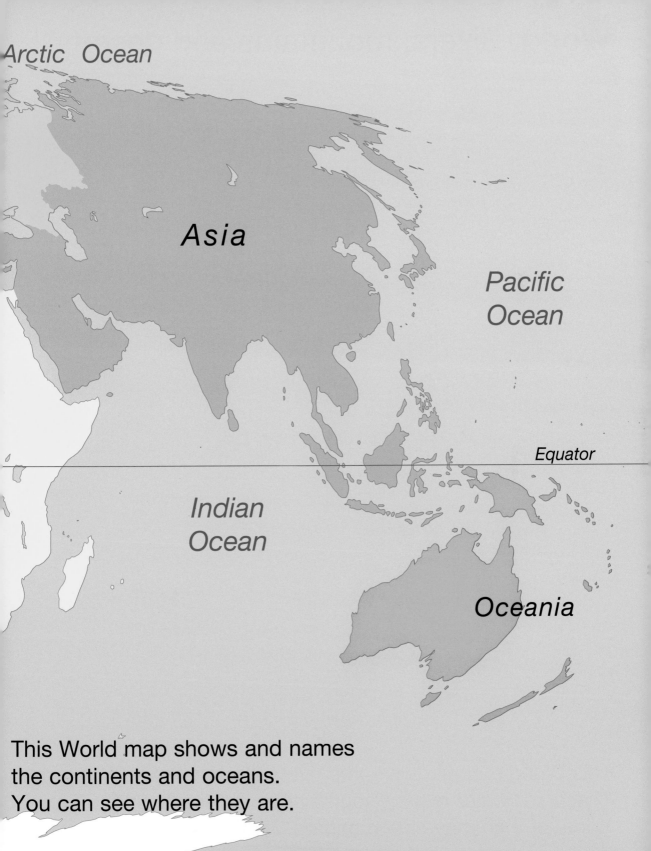

Arctic Ocean

Asia

Pacific
Ocean

Equator

Indian
Ocean

Oceania

This World map shows and names
the continents and oceans.
You can see where they are.

World: Rivers, mountains and deserts

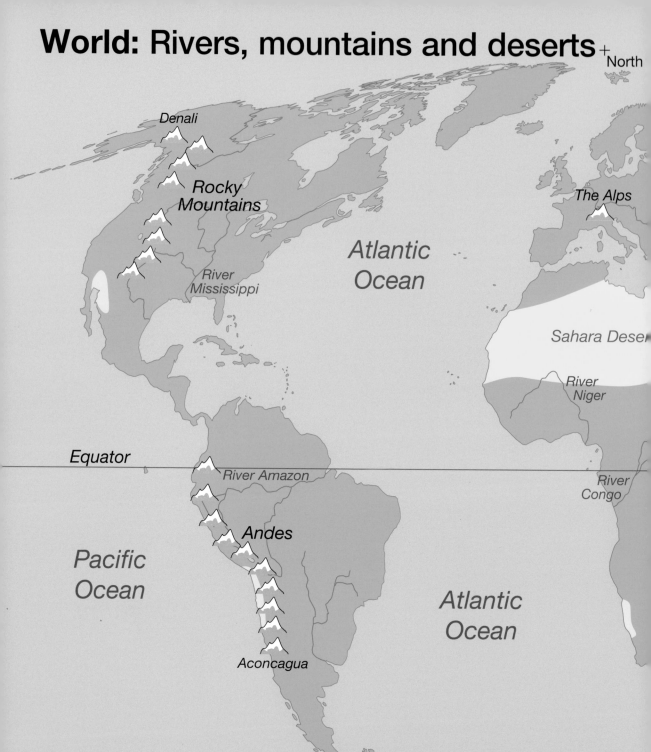

North

Denali

Rocky
Mountains

The Alps

Atlantic
Ocean

Sahara Desert

River
Mississippi

River
Niger

Equator

River Amazon

River
Congo

Andes

Pacific
Ocean

Atlantic
Ocean

Aconcagua

This World map shows some rivers, mountains and deserts.
These are major rivers, mountains and deserts on the Earth.
Some of them have been named.

South Pole

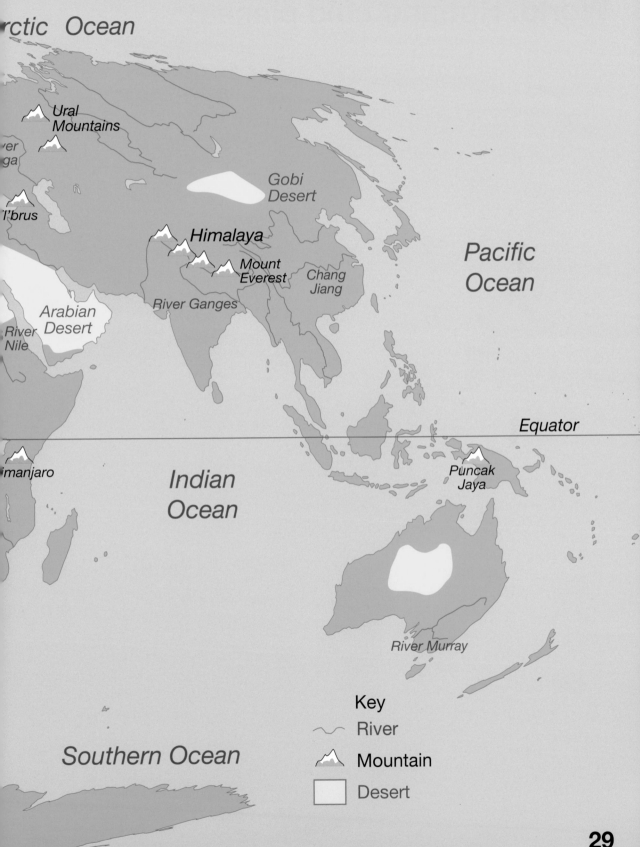

Arctic Ocean

Ural
Mountains

...er
...ga

...l'brus

Gobi
Desert

Himalaya

Mount
Everest

Chang
Jiang

Pacific
Ocean

Arabian
Desert

River Ganges

River
Nile

...manjaro

Indian
Ocean

Equator

Puncak
Jaya

River Murray

Southern Ocean

Key

~ River

⌃ Mountain

☐ Desert

World: Hot and cold places

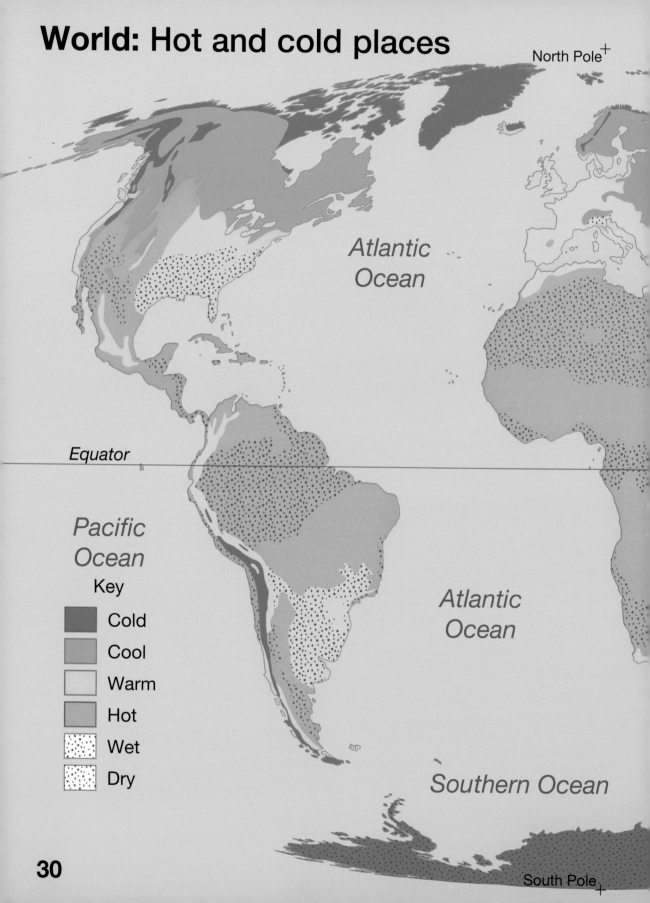

North Pole⁺

Atlantic
Ocean

Pacific
Ocean

Equator

Key

Cold
Cool
Warm
Hot
Wet
Dry

Atlantic
Ocean

Southern Ocean

South Pole

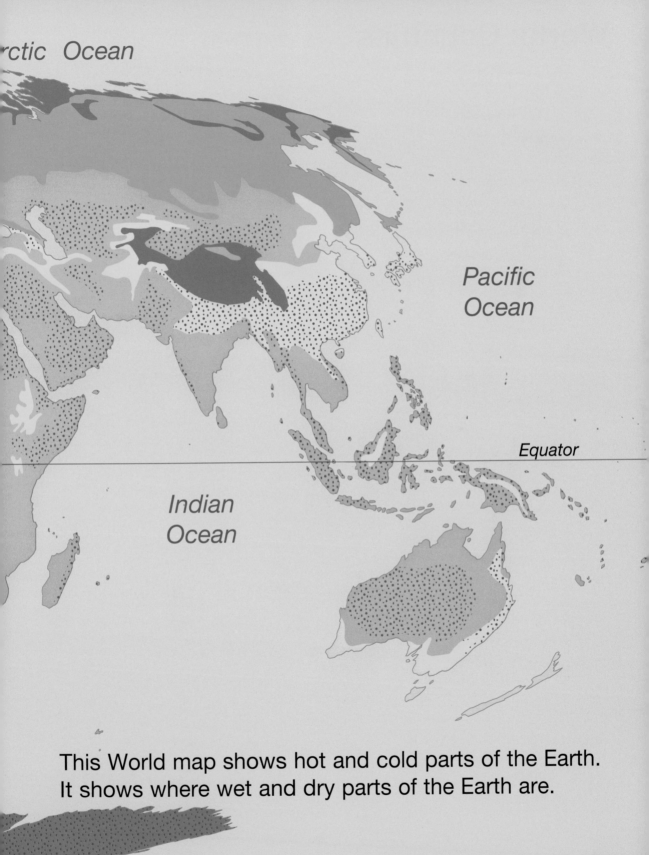

Pacific Ocean

Equator

Indian Ocean

This World map shows hot and cold parts of the Earth. It shows where wet and dry parts of the Earth are.

World: Countries

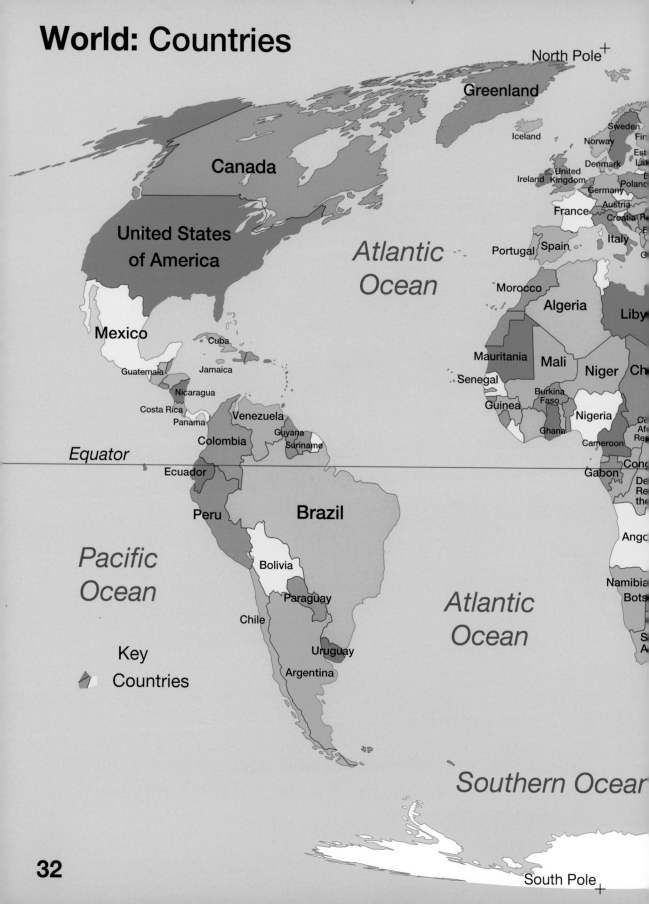

North Pole

Greenland

Canada

Iceland
Sweden
Norway
Denmark
Ireland United Kingdom
Germany
France
Austria
Croatia
Portugal Spain
Italy

United States of America

Morocco

Algeria

Liby

Mexico

Cuba

Jamaica

Guatemala

Nicaragua

Costa Rica
Panama

Venezuela

Colombia

Guyana

Suriname

Mauritania

Mali

Niger

Ch

Senegal

Guinea

Burkina Faso

Nigeria

Ghana

Cameroon

Ce
Af
Re

Atlantic Ocean

Equator

Ecuador

Gabon

Con

De
Re
the

Peru

Brazil

Pacific Ocean

Bolivia

Paraguay

Ang

Chile

Namibia
Bots

Atlantic Ocean

Uruguay

S
A

Argentina

Key

Countries

Southern Ocean

South Pole

32

Russia

Kazakhstan

Mongolia

Japan

Turkmenistan

key

Afghanistan

China

Pacific
Ocean

Iraq

Iran

Pakistan

Nepal

ot

Saudi
Arabia

Oman

India

Bangladesh

Myanmar

Eritrea   Yemen

an

Thailand

Vietnam

Philippines

Ethiopia

Sri
Lanka

Somalia

nda

Malaysia

Kenya

Equator

azania

Indian
Ocean

Indonesia

Papua New
Guinea

Solomon
Islands

ozambique

abwe

Vanuatu

Madagascar

Australia

New
Zealand

This World map shows the countries of the World.
Many countries are named.
Lots of people live in all the countries of the World.

World: Capital cities

North Pole

Nuuk
Reykjavík
Oslo   Hels
Stockl
Dublin   Berlin   War
London
Paris   Vie
Madrid   Rome   S
Lisbon   Athe
Rabat   Algiers
Tripo

Ottawa

Washington

Atlantic Ocean

Havana
Mexico City
Kingston
Guatemala City   Managua
Caracas
San José   Panama City   Georgetown
Bogotá   Paramaribo
Equator
Quito

Nouakchott
Dakar   Bamako   Niamey   Ndjam
Conakry   Abuja
Accra   Bar
Yaoundé
Libreville
Brazzaville
Kinsh
Luanda

Lima
La Paz   Brasília

Pacific Ocean

Sucre

Asunción

Atlantic Ocean

Windhoek
Gabor

Cape Town

Key
Countries
Capital city

Santiago   Buenos Aires   Montevideo

Southern Ocean

South Pole

Arctic Ocean

Pacific Ocean

Indian Ocean

Equator

oscow

Astana

Ulan Bator

kara

Ashgabat

Beijing

hdad

Tehran

Kabul

Islamabad

Tokyo

iro

New
Delhi

Riyadh

Muscat

Dhaka

Hanoi

rtoum

San'a

Nay Pyi Taw

Asmara

Bangkok

Manila

Addis Ababa

Kuala
Lumpur

a

npala

Mogadishu

Nairobi

Jakarta

Dodoma

Port Moresby

Honiara

aka

Antananarivo

Port Vila

arare

Maputo

ria

Canberra

Wellington

A capital city is where the government of a country is based.
Many people live in cities.

A view from space

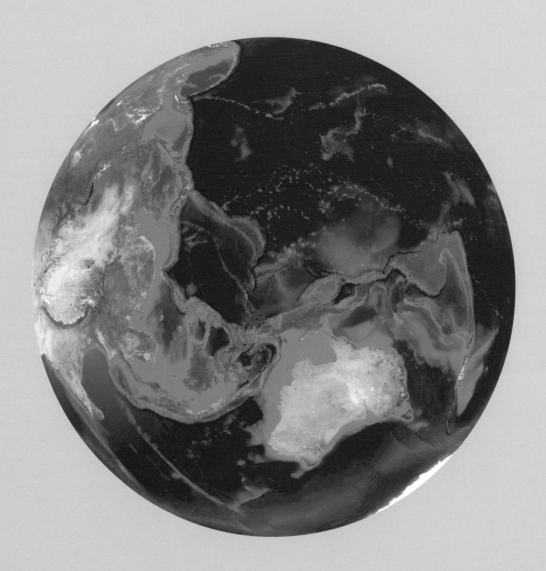

This is a view of the Earth from space.
It shows Oceania and part of Asia as
they look from space.

This is a globe.
A globe is a model of the Earth.

It shows Oceania and part of Asia.
Find the page in the atlas which
shows Asia.
See which part of Asia
the globe shows.
Find Oceania.

Earth's neighbours

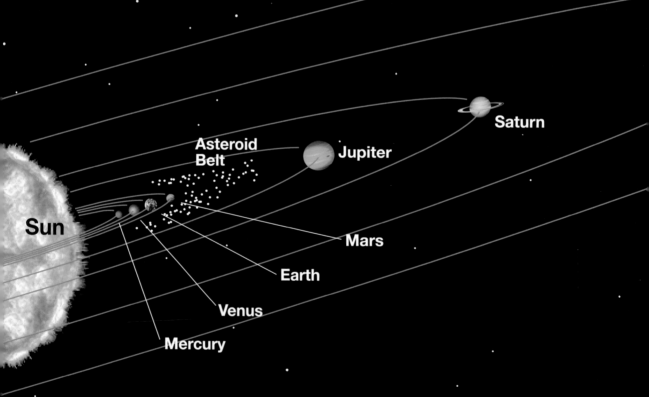

Saturn

Asteroid
Belt

Jupiter

Sun

Mars

Earth

Venus

Mercury

The Sun and its eight planets

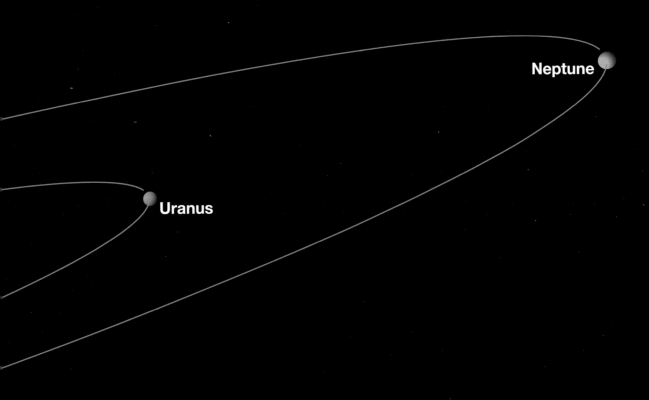

This view shows eight planets that orbit the Sun.
The Earth is the third planet from the Sun.
It is our home.

Index

The Index in an atlas helps you find some of the places named in the atlas.
Use it to look up places.